THE NEED TO KNOW LIBRARY™

EVERYTHING YOU NEED TO KNOW ABOUT
NONBINARY GENDER IDENTITIES

ANITA LOUISE

Rosen
YA™
New York

Published in 2020 by The Rosen Publishing Group, Inc.
29 East 21st Street, New York, NY 10010

Copyright © 2020 by The Rosen Publishing Group, Inc.

First Edition

Library of Congress Cataloging-in-Publication Data

Names: McCormick, Anita Louise, author.
Title: Everything you need to know about nonbinary gender identities / Anita Louise McCormick.
Description: First Edition. | New York : Rosen Publishing, 2020 | Series: The need to know library | Audience: Grades 7–12. | Includes bibliographical references and index.
Identifiers: LCCN 2018047088| ISBN 9781508187622 (library bound) | ISBN 9781508187615 (pbk.)
Subjects: LCSH: Gender identity—Juvenile literature. | Group identity—Juvenile literature.
Classification: LCC HQ1075 .M413 2020 | DDC 305.3—dc23
LC record available at https://lccn.loc.gov/2018047088

Manufactured in the United States of America

CONTENTS

INTRODUCTION

In July 2018, Rebecca Sugar, the creator of the popular cartoon series *Steven Universe*, decided to come out as nonbinary. Up to that point, Sugar had the honor of being the first woman to create an original series for the Cartoon Network. Now Sugar is known as the first openly nonbinary woman to do so.

The term "nonbinary" is a new one for many people. If a person is nonbinary, that means they do not identify as being fully male or female. But there is more to it than that. There are many ways of being nonbinary. Some people who are nonbinary view their gender identity as being partly male and partly female. Some people who are nonbinary feel that at times, they are mostly female, but at other times, they are mostly male. Still other people who are nonbinary feel little, if any, gender identity.

Even though you might not have heard much about them, nonbinary people have existed throughout history. However, many people do not have a clear understanding of what it means to be nonbinary.

This lack of understanding has caused some people who are nonbinary to be misunderstood and bullied. Lack of understanding has also caused problems when it comes to which bathroom to use, how to indicate their gender on documents where male and female are the only choices, and many other situations they deal with every day.

However, there are people working to make things better. The show Rebecca Sugar created, *Steven*

Rebecca Sugar, creator of *Steven Universe,* a popular series on the Cartoon Network, came out as a nonbinary woman in 2018.

Universe, is popular with LGBTQ+ viewers of all ages because some characters are LGBTQ or do not conform to commonly perceived ideas of gender. Creating a show like *Steven Universe* was difficult at a time when TV networks are often criticized by conservative religious and political groups if they include any LGBTQ content in shows intended primarily for children.

But Sugar knew it was worth the effort. In a 2018 interview with *Entertainment Weekly* magazine, Rebecca Sugar stressed the importance of LGBTQ+ visibility in children's programming. "We need to let children know that they belong in this world," she said. "You can't wait to tell them that until after they grow up or the damage will be done."

Experts have found that when children, teens, and even adults have the opportunity to see people like themselves in the TV shows and movies they watch or the books they read, it helps them feel more confident and empowered. Straight white people have had these opportunities every day for many years. In recent years, more TV shows, movies, and books centered on African Americans, Asians, and LGBTQ+ individuals have appeared. Now people who are nonbinary are also starting to have the same opportunities.

If you are exploring your gender identity and think you might be nonbinary, you are not alone. In 2017, a report in *USA Today* used information from the *American Journal of Public Health* to estimate that between 250,000 and 350,000 people in the United States identify as nonbinary. As more people who have a nonbinary gender identity decide to come out, that number is certain to rise.

CHAPTER ONE

WHAT IS GENDER ANYWAY?

The first question most people ask new parents is "Is it a boy or a girl?" Even before a child is born, a doctor can determine the biological sex of a baby by looking at an ultrasound picture of the child in the mother's womb. As soon as the baby is born, the birth gender is recorded and eventually goes on the baby's birth certificate. For most people, the gender they are assigned at birth is the one they identify with throughout their lives.

A BOY OR A GIRL?

Most people do not give much thought to their gender. They were told at an early age they were a boy or a girl, and they never had reason to question this. They grew up feeling comfortable with their assigned gender. In school, they never hesitated when they were asked to mark their gender as "boy" or "girl." They wore the kind of clothes that children of their gender were expected to wear. They also engaged in the kinds of activities

7

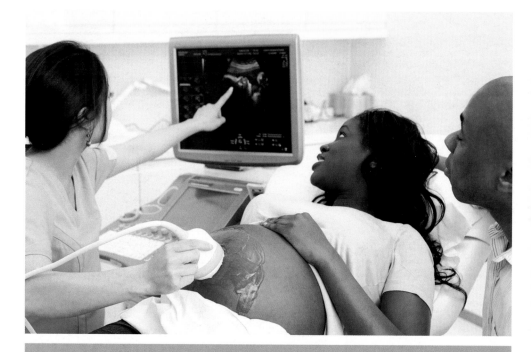

With ultrasound technology, parents can find out the gender of their child months before the baby is born. These parents-to-be may have gender-related expectations for their child.

that were expected for a child of their gender. As they grew older and entered puberty, they felt comfortable with the changes that were happening in their bodies. When they applied for their drivers' licenses, they marked their gender as male or female without giving it a second thought. They also indicated if they were male or female when they applied for jobs. As adults, when they paid their taxes, set up bank accounts, applied for loans, or bought a home, they continued to identify with their birth gender.

However, for some people, the issue of gender is not that simple. While most people feel that that they are male *or* female, this is not true for everyone. Some people do not feel that the idea of being male or female is right for them. These two categories society often uses to describe gender does not describe who they perceive themselves to be. These people see their gender identity as being something other than the gender they were assigned at birth. No matter how many times they were told they were a boy or a girl, that identity did not feel right to them.

If someone's perceived gender identity is different from their biological or birth sex, it is said that they are transgender. The word "transgender" means that a person has a sense of identity that does not correspond

After coming out as transgender, Stiles Zuschlag was asked to leave his religious school. He transferred to a school that was more accepting of his identity, where he was voted homecoming king.

to their birth sex. Some people who are transgender view their gender identity as being completely different from the biological sex they were assigned at birth. They might have been born with the biological sexual characteristics of a female but have the gender identity of being male. Or they might have been born with the biological sexual characteristics of a female but have the gender identity of a male.

Many people think that transgender means having a gender identity that is the opposite of their birth sex. But that is not always the case. For some people who are transgender, their gender perception is something other than, or somewhere in between, male or female.

About one-third of people who are transgender consider themselves to be nonbinary. That means that their gender identity is not strictly male or female. But not all nonbinary people consider themselves to be transgender. Some people who are nonbinary see themselves in a different category from transgender because they have some identification with the sex they were assigned at birth. Whether someone who is nonbinary chooses to call themselves transgender is a personal preference.

As people explore their gender identity and learn more about themselves, they may change the words they use to describe their gender. For example, someone who was born biologically female might at first feel that she is a girl. Then as she matures, she may no longer identify as being fully female and instead, identify as being nonbinary. Later on, they might decide that in addition to being nonbinary, they are gender fluid. In other words, their gender identity is not fixed. At times they may feel more female than male, while at other times they may feel more male than female. At another point in their life, they might decide that the word "transgender" also describes who they are. Like many things in life, learning about your gender identity is an ongoing process.

BIOLOGY, SEXUAL ORIENTATION, AND GENDER IDENTITY

It can be confusing to hear people talk about terms such as biological sex, sexual orientation, and gender identity. There are so many different terms, and new terms for gender identity or sexual attraction seem to be popping up in the media all the time.

Still, there are some basic terms that are almost universally used. Understanding them will help you have a better idea of what people mean when they discuss gender identity or sexual orientation.

Biological sex, or birth sex, has to do with a person's reproductive organs and other biological differences between men and women, such as facial hair, breasts, and the way muscles and fat are distributed on the body. The main terms for this category are male, female, and intersex.

If someone is intersex, they were born with biological characteristics that are both male and female. According to the Intersex Campaign for Equality, up to 1.7 percent of the human population is born with some intersex characteristics. When a baby is born intersex, doctors usually write the biological sex the baby resembles more closely on the birth certificate.

Sexual orientation has to do with whom a person is attracted to. Terms having to do with sexual attraction are gay, straight, lesbian, bisexual, asexual, and pansexual. Gay men are attracted to men. Lesbian women are attracted to women. Straight men are attracted to women. Straight women are attracted to men. Bisexual or pansexual men and women are attracted to both women and men, both transgender and cisgender, as well as nonbinary people. Asexual men and women are not sexually attracted to anyone.

Gender identity is who a person perceives themselves to be. In other words, if someone feels female,

As many schools have become more welcoming toward LGBTQ+ students, many teens have felt safer being open about their sexual orientation.

male, or somewhat male and somewhat female, that is their gender identity. When you hear someone being described as nonbinary, that has to do with their gender identity. Nonbinary is an umbrella term. In other words, it is a term that covers many categories. Some of the gender identities that are categorized as nonbinary are genderqueer, gender fluid, and agender, which means that a person does not identify as any gender.

People who feel comfortable with their assigned sex are cisgender. This means that their gender identity corresponds to their birth sex. Until recent years, most people had not heard the term "cisgender," or "cis" for short. Cis is a Latin word that means "on the side of." Trans means "on the other side of." In other words, if someone is cisgender, that means they are on the side of the gender they were assigned at birth. A German researcher, Volkmar Sigusch, came up with the word in the 1990s when he was studying transgender experiences. At the time, many people used words like "normal" to describe people who were cisgender, which was insulting to anyone who was transgender because it implied that they were not normal.

YOUR GENDER IDENTITY

For many nonbinary people, the thought that their gender is different from their birth sex starts in childhood. Sometimes, the process of questioning gender starts at an early age. Maybe a child decides that the clothes their parents told them to wear do not feel right

Experimenting with clothes and hairstyles to determine what feels right is part of growing up. This is particularly true for nonbinary and transgender young people.

for them. Or maybe they would rather play with toys that most people give to children of a different gender, such as boys wanting to play dress-up with their mother's make-up and clothes or girls casting aside their baby doll to play with toy trucks. Sometimes, these interests in clothes, toys, and activities are a passing curiosity. But other times, it means that a child is not comfortable with their assigned gender.

As transgender and nonbinary children grow, they often find new ways of perceiving and expressing their gender. These include how they dress, how they style their hair, and the hobbies and activities they enjoy.

Being different from what people around you expect can make life difficult. Children who do not identify with their birth gender often experience isolation. This can start when other children or adults in their lives start to notice things about them that make them different from their peers of the same birth gender. If a girl doesn't comply with their idea of what a girl should do, other girls might bully her or ignore her. Sometimes, parents step in and make sure their child is not being bullied. But other times, parents become part of the problem by insisting that their child act like a stereotypical girl or boy.

As difficult as it can be for girls who wear boys' clothing and enjoy toys commonly purchased for boys, it can be even harder for boys who are interested in toys intended for girls and girls' clothing and hairstyles.

The teasing and bullying that transgender and nonbinary children often endure can cause them to feel alienated, anxious, and depressed. Sometimes, it causes them to try to conform to what others expect. Pretending to be

No matter what questions a teen may express about their gender identity, having support from a parent is key.

something they are not can sometimes stop the teasing and bullying. But it often leads to feelings of low self-worth. When a child is being teased, alienated, or isolated at school because of their gender identity, it is very important for parents to step in and let their child know that they are loved and accepted just as they are.

While some people who are nonbinary discover their gender identity during early childhood, others do not begin to question their gender identity until they reach puberty or even later. When children and teens grow up in a family or culture that does not understand or accept the idea of people being LGBTQ+ or nonbinary, they often try to suppress the feeling of not being their assigned gender in order to be accepted. However, nonbinary children and teens who grow up in homes where parents are accepting of LGBTQ+ people and those with nonconforming gender identities are more likely to come out at an early age.

MYTHS AND FACTS

MYTH: Everyone is either male or female.

FACT: There have always been many variations of gender besides male or female. Gender has nothing to do with reproductive organs.

MYTH: Children and teens are too young to understand their gender identity.

FACT: Studies show that even young children have an understanding of what gender means and what is expected of girls and boys. Many people who came out as transgender or nonbinary later in life have early childhood memories of knowing that their gender identity did not match the sex they were assigned at birth.

MYTH: Nonbinary people dress differently from most men or women.

FACT: While some people with nonbinary gender identities choose to have an androgynous appearance, others dress and style their hair in ways that do not set them apart from people with male or female identities. It all depends on how they want to express their gender identity to the world.

CHAPTER TWO

IDENTIFYING AS NONBINARY

The idea that some people are nonbinary is still a new concept to many people. When people with a nonbinary gender identity decide to come out, cisgender people often find it difficult to understand what they are being told. Even people who accept and understand gay, lesbian, and bisexual attraction often have trouble with the idea of someone identifying as something other than male or female.

MOVING BEYOND CULTURAL NORMS

For many years, society in general has thought of the human population as binary. In other words, there are boys, and there are girls. There are women, and there are men. At an early age, most boys and girls were taught what kind of clothes they are expected to wear, what their interests should be, and how they should behave. If they went outside of these norms, girls were often called tomboys, and boys were called sissies.

Fortunately, in recent years, ideas of how males and females should behave have evolved. While some religious and cultural groups still believe that men and women should act and dress in certain ways, overall, there are fewer absolutes. This change in attitude has brought about an increased acceptance of people who do not fit into the cultural norms of male and female.

Despite this greater sensitivity to differences in gender expression, the idea of a person having a gender that is neither male or female can be hard for some to understand. When people have spent their entire lives thinking that

The teen years are an important time to figure out who you want to be and how you want the world to see you.

everyone is either male or female, the idea of someone being something other than male or female can be hard to grasp. This confusion can cause even well-intentioned people to say things that are hurtful to nonbinary people. Comments such as "How can anyone not be a male or a female?"can cut someone to the core.

THE TELEVISION SET

In the past, few openly nonbinary characters appeared in movies or on television. But as the entertainment industry's awareness of nonbinary people increases, things are changing for the better.

Asia Kate Dillon, an American actor who plays Taylor Mason on the Showtime series *Billions*, made history when they became the first person with a nonbinary gender identity to portray a nonbinary character on an American television series. In 2018, Dillon was nominated for Best Supporting Actor at the Critic's Choice Award.

Dillon uses the pronouns "they/them" (instead of "he/his" or "she/hers") and feels honored to have the opportunity to play a character with a nonbinary identity. In a 2018 interview with Yahoo Lifestyle, Dillon said, "I spent so many years not understanding my own gender identity, not having the language to talk about it, and not feeling safe in many environments to talk about it. And so now, having the opportunity to talk about it and have it printed is extraordinary for me, and it doesn't get tiring."

While they are not necessarily identified as nonbinary, other TV shows feature characters that don't identify as male or female. The long-running British TV series *Doctor Who* is one example. *Doctor Who* is a Time Lord — a human-appearing alien that can travel through time and space. A 2017 *Entertainment Weekly* article reported that when another character on the show asked Doctor Who about their gender, they replied, "We're billions of years beyond your petty human obsession with gender and its associated stereotypes."

Since the beginning of the series, the character of Doctor Who has been played by a series of male actors. But in 2018, for the first time, the role was played by a female actor, Jodie Whittaker.

In 2016, Jodie Whittaker became the first female actor to play Doctor Who, a nonbinary alien who travels through time and space.

MANY WAYS OF BEING NONBINARY

Nonbinary is an umbrella term for many different gender identities. Gender is actually a broad spectrum of identities. While there can be as many ways to be nonbinary as there are people, there are some commonly used terms for nonbinary identities that describe a person's gender identity more clearly than just saying that they are nonbinary.

When someone is gender fluid, they feel more feminine on some days and more masculine on other days. If someone is agender, they do not see themselves as male or female. A demiboy or a demiguy sees themselves as somewhat male but not fully a man. A demigirl or demigal sees themselves as somewhat female but not fully a woman. If someone says they are genderqueer, they want to identify in a way that does not limit them to being male or female.

Sometimes when someone discovers that they are nonbinary, they experiment with different terms for expressing their gender identity. If one way of describing your gender identity does not feel right, you can always try another way.

UNDERSTANDING TAKES TIME

Many people confuse ideas and terms about gender identity with words that describe whom someone is attracted to. For example, if someone says that a person is nonbinary, some people might confuse it with being bisexual, which means that someone is attracted to both men and women. Or they might confuse being agender—someone who has no gender identity—with being asexual, which means someone who does not feel sexually attracted to other people.

Some people may also confuse the idea of being nonbinary with being intersex. If a person is intersex, they have both male and female biological sexual characteristics. Just like anyone else, an intersex person can be male, female, transgender, or nonbinary.

A person who is nonbinary can have a male body, a female body, or an intersex body. A transgender person who has used hormones and/or had surgery to change their body to be more conforming to their gender identity can also be nonbinary.

Some nonbinary people look somewhat androgynous, meaning it is difficult for people to know if they are male or female. But many nonbinary people look no different from someone whose gender identity is male or female. It is impossible to know for sure what someone's gender identity is based solely on appearance.

If you are feeling a bit confused, don't be embarrassed. Even people like TV show host Ellen DeGeneres, who publicly announced that she is a lesbian in 1997, found that she

After Asia Kate Dillon came out as nonbinary, they did media interviews to help educate the public about nonbinary gender identity.

had things to learn about nonbinary gender identities. In an interview with nonbinary actor Asia Kate Dillon on *The Ellen Show*, DeGeneres admitted, "It's really confusing, and I think people assume just because I'm gay I understand all of this and I don't." By admitting she did not know everything about being nonbinary and asking Dillon questions, she helped to educate everyone who was watching.

NONBINARY ACCEPTANCE IN OTHER CULTURES

Identifying as something other than male or female is still new to many people in our American culture. But that is not true in other cultures and in other parts of the world. As far back as 400 BCE, nonbinary people were recognized in Hindu literature.

In North America, many Native American tribes recognize and honor nonbinary individuals. They often have special roles in society, such as spiritual leaders others come to for support and advice. Sometimes, they are called two-spirit. Two-spirit, or nonbinary individuals, are often valued in tribal societies for their abilities to understand issues from both a male and female perspective. In some Native American tribes any member that is LGBTQ+ is called two-spirit and is welcome to take part in Two-spirit activities, pow wows, and rituals.

Geo Soctomah Neptune identifies as two-spirit and is a member of the Passamaquoddy tribe in Maine. When

Geo was a small child, elders in the tribe told Geo's family that Geo was two-spirit. In traditional Passamaquoddy culture, people who are two-spirit are valued for the spiritual roles they play in tribal society. At first, Geo's family had a difficult time accepting the idea that their child had a nonbinary two-spirit identity because this was not in line with the family's Catholic beliefs. But as time went on, they realized that what the elders said was true. Geo, known as George at the time, was not male—Geo was two-spirit!

In Passamaquoddy culture, men usually weave plain baskets, while women weave the fancy baskets that are often seen in Native American markets and museums. When Geo was four years old, their grandmother Molly Neptune Parker, an award-winning fancy basket weaver, became Geo's teacher. Geo's grandmother specialized in weaving fancy baskets, so that is what she taught. Geo enjoyed weaving fancy baskets and earned the title of Master Basket Weaver at twenty years old. Neptune's work often wins awards at Native American basket festivals. Neptune especially enjoys weaving rainbow-colored baskets because the bright colors represent LGBTQ+ and their two-spirit identity.

Weaving fancy baskets is only one way that Neptune expresses their nonbinary two-spirit identity. Neptune also does drag performances using the name Lyzz Bien. During their drag performances, Neptune likes to wear clothing and accessories that were created by Native American designers.

In a 2016 interview with John Paul Brammer for NBC News, Neptune said, "We [two-spirit people] balance two polarities, two energies in our bodies,

David Young, a member of the Two-Spirit Society, prepares an altar for a healing ceremony. Many Native American tribes recognize the importance of their LGBTQ+ members.

two energies in the same spiritual place." "Those two polarities are not supposed to be able to coexist, but that's why two-spirit people exist. We bring them into balance."

A VITAL EDUCATION

The process of educating society about nonbinary gender identity is still in its early stages. In March 2017, CBSN aired a groundbreaking report titled, "Gender—The Space Between." In this documentary, the reporters explained that there is more to the gender spectrum than male and female. According to the documentary description, "There is a type of transgender person you never hear about. They are called nonbinary. They use the pronouns they/them. And they do not identify with being either a man or a woman. Rather, these individuals often choose to reject gender completely, or fluctuate between masculinity and femininity on a day-to-day basis."

The documentary interviewed many people with transgender and nonbinary identities and gave them the opportunity to discuss their experiences. They talked about how they felt when they first realized they were nonbinary and how their gender identity affected their lives. The participants, many of them young adults, talked about how people in their lives reacted when they were told about their loved one's gender identity. The interviewees also discussed problems they experienced when members of their family or peers and teachers at school did not understand.

Even with the effort to educate the public, it will likely take some time before people who identify as nonbinary will be fully accepted and understood. But as long as parents, teachers, friends, and community members do their best to keep an open mind, they can offer valuable support to someone who is coming out as nonbinary.

CHAPTER THREE

CLAIMING YOUR NONBINARY IDENTITY

Like everyone else, nonbinary people want to be recognized and accepted for who they are. This is often a challenge, as our society is still in the process of understanding what it means to be something other than male or female. Even if someone who is nonbinary usually has a wardrobe and hairstyle that might make others think they are male or female, people who are openly nonbinary don't want to be labeled with the wrong identity, or misgendered.

WHY IDENTITY MATTERS

Many people do not understand what it means for someone to be nonbinary, so they don't even think there is a gender option outside of male or female. Even well-meaning people may wonder why people with a nonbinary identity don't just accept being labeled as male or female. The reason is simple: those words do not describe who they are. Also, if someone thinks you are a male or a female, that often comes with a set of stereotypes and expectations that are often different from how you feel about yourself.

Some people with nonbinary gender identities dress and style their hair in the way you would expect a male or female to appear. Because of this, many people assume that is their gender identity. Even when nonbinary people present as androgynous, in other words, they present in a way that combines dress or hairstyles of boys and girls, many people still assume they have a binary identity.

Nonbinary youth who present as androgynous or as a gender other than their birth gender are less likely to be misgendered than those who present primarily as their birth sex. However, because they appear to be presenting in a way that is different from their birth sex, they are more likely to be bullied or harassed. Bullying can cause many serious problems, especially if those in authority, such as teachers and parents do nothing to stop it. These problems include depression, anxiety, and suicidal thoughts.

Misgendering by people who only think in terms

When nonbinary and transgender teens are bullied, it can cause serious problems such as anxiety, depression, and suicidal thoughts.

of male and female is one of the universal problems that people who are nonbinary must deal with. Yan Logan, a software engineering student who identifies as being nonbinary, explained it this way in their article on Medium (www.medium.com) titled "Why being a non-binary is tough." "It's really sad to think that people try to put you and your actions in some sort of *explainable, familiar* terms," they wrote. "Even if they are pretty educated and intelligent, still most of them will see you as a male or a female. They might completely accept your trans-identity, but you still will be seen as 'that guy' and 'that girl.'"

NONBINARY PRONOUNS

Getting people to use the correct pronoun is a very common issue for nonbinary youth. Some people who discover they have nonbinary gender identities continue to go by he/him or she/her pronouns. But others prefer to use pronouns that are gender neutral. That means the pronouns do not refer to male or female.

"They/them" is one of the more common pronouns nonbinary people ask others to use. "They" or "them" is used in place of "he/him" or "she/her." For example, "Terry could not come, but maybe we will see them at our next meeting." For some people, it might sound awkward at first to use "they/them" when referring to one person instead of a group. But with practice, it sounds more natural and becomes easier. There are also other, less familiar gender-neutral pronouns that some nonbinary people choose to use, such as "ze," "hir," and "hirs."

If you are nonbinary and have decided to change your pronouns, it will probably take some time before everyone remembers to use the right words. If they forget and use your old pronouns, the best thing to do is gently remind them of the change.

NONBINARY PRIDE FLAGS

Just like other groups in the LGBT community, nonbinary people use pride flags to celebrate their identity. They often use these flags in pride parades and events. Some nonbinary people like to display the rainbow-colored pride flag, which celebrates the entire LGBTQ+ community. It is a flag that almost everyone recognizes.

In addition to the pride flag, other flags have been created to celebrate various nonbinary gender identities. The transgender flag was designed by Monica Helms, a trans woman, in 1999. It has blue, pink, and white stripes. The blue represents male, the pink represents female, and the white represents people who are nonbinary or intersex, as well as people who are in the process of transitioning.

In 2011, Marilyn Roxie created a new pride flag to celebrate genderqueer and nonbinary individuals. This flag has three stripes: purple, white, and chartreuse green. The chartreuse green stripe represents people who are

(continued on the next page)

(continued from the previous page)

outside of the gender binary of male and female. The white stripe represents people who are agender, or gender neutral. The purple stripe represents people who are a mix of, or in between, male and female.

Then in 2014, seventeen-year-old Kye Rowan created a nonbinary flag for people who did not feel that the transgender or the genderqueer flags adequately represented their gender identity. The flag has four stripes. The yellow represents anyone whose gender is outside of the binary. The white stripe represents many, or all, genders. The purple stripe represents anyone who feels their gender is a mix of male and female, and the black stripe represents people who feel they are without gender, or gender neutral.

The nonbinary flag, with its yellow, white, purple, and black stripes, represents the diverse spectrum of nonbinary gender identities. The flag is often seen at Pride parades and other LGBTQ+ events.

NONBINARY IDENTITY ON LEGAL DOCUMENTS

If your gender identity is the same as your birth sex, you will have no problem when it comes to indicating your gender identity on legal documents. But openly transgender and nonbinary people do not have it so easy. Most documents have only two boxes you can check: one for male, and the other for female.

Some nonbinary people choose to continue using their birth sex on documents such as drivers' licenses, birth certificates, passports, documents at work, and so on. They have decided that it's easier to mark an option that is already on the form, especially if their clothes, hairstyle, and physical characteristics correspond to their birth sex.

However, other nonbinary people are tired of having to mark down a gender identity that is not really theirs. They want to have the option of identifying as something other than male or female. This is especially true of nonbinary people who look androgynous, meaning without sexual characteristics that allow people to easily identify them as a man or a woman. This is also true of nonbinary people who choose to present, or wear clothes and hairstyles, in a way that makes them look like a gender different from their birth gender.

Throughout the years, many transgender and nonbinary people have had problems with police, airport officials, and other law enforcement personnel because the gender identity on their documents does not match the gender they are presenting as. There are nonbinary people who have taken legal action to make their right to identify as something other than male or female available to themselves, as well as to others.

NONBINARY DRIVERS

Some states have passed laws that give people the option of marking a box labeled "X" as their gender on legal documents such as their driver's license and birth certificate. Gaining the right to be identified as something other than male or female on legal documents has been a long struggle. But fortunately, progress is now

Dana Zzyym, an intersex Navy veteran, was denied a US passport because they refused to check either male or female on the application form. Zzyym sued the State Department and won the right to be issued a passport.

being made. In 2016, Oregon became the first state to allow drivers to have this option.

Changing your gender identity on legal documents is becoming easier than it once was, although the legal fees can be expensive. This is especially true if you live in a state or province where the laws that say people must identify as the gender they were assigned at birth have not yet been challenged.

CELEBRATING PRIDE

Many LGBTQ+ people and their allies enjoy participating in pride celebrations. Pride celebrations often include a parade in which brightly colored rainbow flags and clothing can be seen. LGBTQ+ pride is one way people can take a stand against discrimination and violence against the community, as well as promote pride and dignity for those in the community. It is a time to celebrate not only sexual diversity, but gender variance, such as being transgender or nonbinary as well.

In addition to Pride Month celebrations in June, other days, weeks, and months have been designated as LGBT holidays, or days of commemoration, including the following:

- May 17 is International Day Against Homophobia and Transphobia.
- March 31 is International Transgender Day of Visibility.

(continued on the next page)

(continued from the previous page)

- **The last week of March is National GLBT Health Awareness Week.**
- **July 14 is International Nonbinary Day. This date was selected because it is halfway between International Woman's Dan and International Men's Day.**
- **October is LGBTQ History Month.**

Pride parades are a fun way for people in the LGBTQ+ community to come together and celebrate their diverse sexual orientations and gender identities.

FACEBOOK OFFERS MORE GENDER OPTIONS

Being able to identify as their true gender on social media is important to many people with a nonbinary identity. In February 2014, Facebook realized that not all of

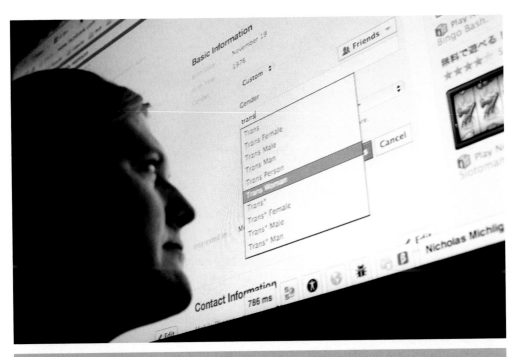

Recognizing that not all of their users identified as male or female, in 2014 Facebook began offering a range of gender identity options on the social media platform.

their users identify as male or female. So they decided to start offering dozens of nonbinary gender alternatives to "male" or "female" to their users. Ari Chivukula, a software engineer who identifies as transgender, was part of the Facebook team that made the decision to include such a large number of gender identity options. Chivukula hopes this change will help society become more accepting of people who do not identify as male or female.

CHAPTER FOUR

FINDING SUPPORT

Like other members of the LGBTQ+ community, nonbinary students benefit from having supportive people around them. It can sometimes be difficult for any teenager to navigate the world of school, society, and home. If a teenager is transgender or nonbinary, there are often more struggles with bullying, anxiety, and depression.

Of course, support at home is very important. If a nonbinary teenager's parents support them in being open about their gender identity, it makes life much easier. Understanding gender is a process, and there is much to learn for everyone in the family.

When parents learn that their child or teenager is nonbinary, it might take them some time to adjust. The concept of someone not being male or female is a new concept to many parents. If they are being asked to use different pronouns or even a different name, they are likely to make mistakes at times and use the wrong words.

FITTING INTO SOCIETY

Nonbinary people may struggle to figure out where they fit into the predominately male and female social structures of our society. In school, at work, and in other social settings, males and females are often expected to behave and socialize in different ways. These situations can be challenging for nonbinary people. They often struggle to try and fit in to one gender group or another. Often, they end up socializing with the group that is the closest match to their gender identity, such as someone whose identity is more female than male socializing as a woman. If there are a large number of LGBTQ+ students in a school, nonbinary youth often make people from that group an important part of their social circle.

When openly transgender or nonbinary youth

ALL GENDER RESTROOM
ANYONE CAN USE THIS RESTROOM
REGARDLESS OF GENDER IDENTITY
OR EXPRESSION

When all-gender restrooms are available in public spaces, nonbinary and transgender people are no longer forced to choose between restrooms marked "Men" or "Women."

want to participate on athletic teams, cheerleading squads, and other activities that are sometimes restricted to being for boys or girls, it also presents challenges for students who do not identify as being fully male or female.

Deciding which bathroom to use can be a problem, especially for nonbinary students who present as androgynous or as the opposite of their birth gender.

Sometimes, the best way to deal with this is to talk to a teacher, principal, or school board member. If you need additional help, you might want to contact LGBTQ+ organizations, diversity groups, or legal services and see what advice they can offer.

COMING OUT OR STAYING IN

Not all people who discover they have a nonbinary gender identity choose to be open about it. An issue every nonbinary person must deal with is deciding if, when, and how to come out to those around them. Anyone who is thinking about coming out hopes that friends and family will be understanding and not judge or mock their gender identity. It helps if you know that the people you are thinking about coming out to are open minded and accepting of LGBTQ+ people. Still, for many, there is the fear that while someone you know might accept the idea of someone else being transgender or nonbinary, if they find out that you are transgender or nonbinary, will they treat you differently?

While some relatives may be fine with the idea of a family member being nonbinary, others might hold on to religious or cultural beliefs that make it hard for them to be supportive. Sometimes, people choose to come out to some family members but not to others. Or they choose to come out gradually, starting with people they feel will be most understanding and supportive.

Sometimes, friends or family members accidentally "out" someone because they assume that if you told them, you also told other people. When someone tells you they are nonbinary or LGBTQ+, you should not tell anyone without their permission. Otherwise, they might be thrown into a situation that they are not yet ready to deal with.

When people discover they are nonbinary after they become an adult, it can be liberating as well as scary. While they no longer are required to live with a gender identity that is not accurate or live their life in a way their parents, school authorities, classmates, or religious institutions expect, they still must go through the process of figuring out whom they want to tell and how they want to tell them. As with younger people who realize they are nonbinary, adults who discover they have a nonbinary gender identity are often concerned about how this might affect their lives going forward.

SUPPORT GROUPS AT SCHOOL

Support groups are a great place to find others who are going through similar life experiences. Some teens decide to talk to their parents first when they decide to come out. However, if teens fear that their parents' beliefs will keep them from accepting their nonbinary identity, they sometimes start the process of coming out with a trusted friend, teacher, or counselor.

Many schools have gay-straight alliances (GSAs). A GSA is a support group where members of the LGBTQ+ community can feel safe talking about whatever challenges they may be facing in their lives. A GSA is intended for both LGBTQ+ and straight students, so people outside the group don't necessarily know if members are LGBTQ+ or coming to offer support to friends who are.

Gay-straight alliances (GSAs) are a great place for those who are LGBTQ+ or exploring their gender identity or sexual orientation to feel safe and supported.

Even if your school does not have an LGBTQ+ support group, they might have a diversity group that you can join. Diversity groups often have a wide focus and help support not only LGBTQ+ students, but also students from diverse racial, social, and ethnic groups.

In addition to school groups, some local LGBTQ+ groups offer activities and support for LGBTQ+ youth in their community. PFLAG (formerly also known as Parents, Family & Friends of Lesbians and Gays) is one national organization that is working to help LGBTQ+ youth with peer support, education, and advocacy. They are a grassroots organization that has more than four hundred local chapters. You can check their website (http://www.pflag.org) to see if they have a branch in your area.

BEING LGBTQ+ IN RURAL AREAS

Even under the best of circumstances, trying to understand your nonbinary gender identity and deciding how and when to come out can be challenging. But youth who live in rural areas or in areas where there is a lack of understanding about LGBTQ+ and nonbinary issues often have a more difficult time finding support. In addition, rural areas are not as likely to have support groups for LGBTQ students.

For many nonbinary and LGBTQ+ youth, the internet has been an invaluable resource for finding information and support. While it is ideal to be able to find support in your own community, the internet offers valuable information for anyone who wants to learn more about their gender identity and find support.

While it is important to keep internet safety rules in mind and never give out your address or other personal information, the internet is a great way to find supportive friends who are experiencing the same things you are.

TrevorSpace (https://www.trevorspace.org) is a social networking website for LGBTQ+ youth and their allies ages thirteen to twenty-four. This website offers a safe space to discuss things such as coming out, gender identity, family, relationships, transitioning, and sexual orientation. It is run by the Trevor Project, a suicide prevention hotline for LGBTQ+ youth.

Anyone thirteen years and older can sign up for a Facebook account and ask to join the member-run nonbinary groups. Most nonbinary Facebook groups are private, meaning comments you write in these groups are visible only to other group members. Twitter, Tumblr, Instagram, and other social networking sites also offer opportunities for nonbinary members to connect.

NONBINARY VLOGGERS

Watching and connecting with vloggers is one way many nonbinary and LGBTQ+ people share their experiences and form a sense of community. A quick search on You-Tube will turn up many vlogs where channel hosts and their friends talk about the nonbinary experience.

Ashley Wylde is one of the best-known nonbinary vloggers. Wylde started her video channel to share her experiences and connect with other people on the nonbinary gender spectrum. In June 2015, Ashley started the Gender Tag Project to encourage people all over the world to share their experiences with gender. Wylde started this project on her You-Tube channel by posting a "tag" video that offered ten prompts having to do with a person's gender. The goal was to help people think about and better understand not only their gender, but also how and why they present their gender as they do and their gender roles in society. This video project was meant to create a better public understanding of gender. By fall 2018, more than one thousand people have chosen to share their experiences by posting Gender Tag videos. Because of her work with the Gender Tag Project, Wylde was invited to give a TEDx Talk about the importance of authentic gender expression.

Ashley Wylde is a popular YouTube vlogger whose channel has helped many nonbinary teens and young adults explore their gender identity.

FINDING SUPPORT FOR GENDER DYSPHORIA AND TRANSITIONING

While not all people with nonbinary identities experience gender dysphoria, many do. Gender dysphoria is the unease or distress that transgender and nonbinary people experience because their gender identity does not match the sex and gender they were assigned at birth.

Gender dysphoria can range from mild to severe. It can range from a mild dislike or disassociation from a sex-related physical characteristic, such as breasts or a penis, to severe dislike. Gender dysphoria is one of the main reasons transgender people feel depressed, anxious, or even suicidal.

Another way nonbinary and transgender people experience dysphoria is when people misgender them—in other words, they call them words that have to do with a different gender than they are.

Some people deal with gender dysphoria in ways that do not require medical intervention. This method may work as long as the dysphoria is not severe enough to have a major impact on their lives. For example, some nonbinary and transgender people who were assigned a female identity at birth feel some level of dysphoria about their breasts. To help with this issue, they were sports bras instead of cupped bras to make their chest appear as flat as possible. Other transgender and nonbinary people wear binders, which are similar to a sports bra, but compress their breasts even tighter.

Sometimes when teens are experiencing gender dysphoria, doctors prescribe medicine that inhibits, or slows down, the onset of puberty by blocking hormones, Drugs that block hormones are called GnRH agonists. These drugs can temporarily slow the development of secondary sexual characteristics, such as breasts and facial hair. When the medicine is stopped, puberty resumes.

Medical transitioning can involve taking hormones and having surgery so the person's body will more closely conform to their gender identity. Transitioning can help a person whose gender identity is different from their assigned sex feel more comfortable in their

For nonbinary teens, gender dysphoria can range from a manageable annoyance to a serious problem that requires professional help.

body. As with any medical procedure, there are risks involved, and the process is expensive. While many health insurance companies now cover gender reassignment surgery and hormone treatment, not all do.

If you are experiencing gender dysphoria, it is a good idea to talk with a therapist who has experience in helping nonbinary youth. They can help you navigate through the various options you may want to consider.

HOW TO BE A GOOD ALLY

If a friend or family member tells you they are nonbinary, it is important to offer understanding and support. The following are some tips about how to be a good ally:

1. Let them know you are available to listen as they go through the process of understanding more about their gender identity.
2. Do not accidentally "out" them to anyone. Just because someone confides in you does not mean they have told their parents, teachers, or other students.
3. Ask which pronouns they use. If you accidentally use the wrong pronoun, apologize.
4. Do not ask direct questions about things they might not be ready to discuss. For example, do not ask a nonbinary person if they are planning to transition with hormones or surgery.
5. If they have chosen to use a different name than their

birth name because they believe it better represents their gender, remember to use it.

6. Be patient and encouraging as your friend goes through the process of deciding how they want to present. Many nonbinary people do a lot of experimenting with clothing, hair, and other elements of presentation before they find what feels right for them.

7. Offer to go to GSA meetings or those of another organization with your friend.

8. When you hear anyone teasing, bullying, or making inappropriate jokes about LGBTQ+ people, take a stand. If it is a situation you do not feel safe becoming involved with, talk to a teacher or your parents about it.

9. Recommend any support resources you may be aware of in the community.

FREEDOM TO BE YOURSELF

The process of understanding your nonbinary gender and coming out to others is often challenging. But in the end, it can also be a very rewarding experience. In an interview with Anna Goldfarb of Vice.com. Dill Werner, a science fiction and fantasy author, explained how their life is better now that they decided to come out as nonbinary: "I'm much happier now. I spent too long making everyone else happy by portraying myself as someone I wasn't. Coming out as nonbinary wasn't easy. Many of my long-time binary lesbian and gay friends didn't believe it was real. Their disbelief gave me the courage

When nonbinary and transgender teens feel safe and accepted, they can focus on other areas of their lives, such as taking part in fun and healthy activities with their friends.

to speak up for myself. I'd been pretending before. *This was the real me.*"

If you find that you are nonbinary, your journey of self-discovery will likely take many twists and turns. Every person's journey in learning about their gender identity and how they want to express it in the world is different. But each step of the journey will bring you more understanding of your true identity and more freedom to be yourself.

10 GREAT QUESTIONS TO ASK A COUNSELOR

1. How can I be sure I'm nonbinary?
2. What is the best way to come out to my family?
3. Can you recommend some good support resources in my community?
4. How do I know if I should use the women's or men's bathroom?
5. How should I go about changing my gender identity on school records?
6. What should I do when people use the wrong pronoun or misgender me?
7. Does my primary care physician need to know that I am nonbinary?
8. How can I find a church, synagogue, or other spiritual group that will be accepting?
9. How should I deal with people who do not accept my nonbinary identity?
10. I am thinking about transitioning when I am older. Whom can I turn to for advice?

agender A person who does not identify as any particular gender.

androgynous Possessing a combination of male and female characteristics.

assigned gender The gender a baby is assigned at birth, based on genitalia.

binary Involving two things or possibilities.

bisexual A person who is attracted to both women and men.

demiboy A nonbinary person who identifies partly, but not completely, as male.

demigirl A nonbinary person who identifies partly, but not completely, as female.

gender dysphoria The distress some people experience because the biological sex they were assigned at birth is different from their gender identity.

gender fluid Describing a nonbinary person who does not have a fixed gender identity and alternates between feeling male and female.

gender identity A person's sense of their own gender.

hormone therapy A medical treatment that helps a transgender or nonbinary person appear more like their gender identity.

intersex To have genitalia and other physical characteristics that are both male and female.

misgender To call someone the wrong gender.

present To display one's gender through clothing, hairstyle, speech, and other self-expression.

stereotypes Beliefs that are widely held, but not necessarily true.

transgender Describes someone whose gender identity is different from the sex they were assigned at birth.

transition The process of changing one's gender presentation and/or sex characteristics to conform to one's gender identity.

two-spirit A Native American term for tribe members who are nonbinary or LGBTQ+

umbrella term A word that covers a wide range of concepts or options.

vlogger Someone who records and posts videos on a regular basis for an internet audience.

Gender Spectrum
1501 Powell Street, Suite H
Emeryville, CA 94608
(510) 788-4412
Website: https://www.genderspectrum.org
Facebook and Twitter: @GenderSpectrum
Instagram @gender_spectrum
YouTube: @genderspectrum
Gender Spectrum works to make the world more inclu-
    sive for children and teens of all genders. They work
    with families, institutions, schools, and other orga-
    nizations to expand their understanding of gender
    and gender-related issues.

GLAAD
5455 Wilshire Bouelvard, #1500
Los Angeles, CA 90036
(323) 933-2240
Website: http://www.glaad.org
Facebook, Instagram, and Twitter: @glaad
GLAAD has been working for the acceptance of LGBT
    individuals since 1985. Their work includes push-
    ing for antidiscrimination laws and public education
    about issues that affect the LGBT community.

GLSEN
110 William Street, 30th Floor
New York, NY 10038
(212) 727-0135

Website:// https://www.glsen.org
Facebook: @GLSEN and @gaystraightalliances
Instagram and Twitter @glsen
GLSEN helps create safe, affirming schools that allow K–12 LGBTQ+ students to thrive without fear of bullying or harassment. The website offers resources including information on starting and running gay-straight alliance programs.

Human Rights Campaign (HRC)
1640 Rhode Island Avenue NW
Washington, DC 20036-3278
(800) 777-4723
Website: https://www.hrc.org
Facebook and Instagram @humanrightscampaign
Twitter: @HRC
HRC is the largest LGBTQ+ civil rights group in the United States. They work to ensure and expand civil rights for all LGBTQ+ people.

LGBT Youth Allies
Website: http://www.youthallies.com
Facebook: @LGBTYouthAllies
Twitter: @youthallies
LGBT Youth Allies is a project that supports LGBT youth, as well as their families and allies. The website provides a list of links to organizations and resources.

LGBT Youth Line
PO Box 73118, Wood Street PO

Toronto, ON, M4Y 2W5
Canada
(416) 962-2232
Website: http://www.youthline.ca
Facebook and Instagram: @lgbtyouthline
Twitter: @LGBTYouthLine
LGBT Youth Line is a youth-led organization that helps LGBT and two-spirit youth in Ontario through anonymous peer support, resources, and training.

Positive Space Network
504 Iroquois Shore Road, Unit 12A
Oakville, ON
Canada
(905) 878-9785
Website: https://www.positivespacenetwork.ca
Facebook: @positivespacenetworkCA
Twitter: @PSN_HALTON
Instagram: @PSN.HALTON/
Positive Space Network provides education, awareness, visibility, and support programs for LGBTQ+ youth. The site also offers a 24/7 crisis hotline.

Trans Lifeline
101 Broadway, #311
Oakland, CA 94607
USA: (877) 565-8860
Canada: (877) 330-6366
https://www.translifeline.org
Facebook, Instagram, and Twitter: @TransLifeline
A grassroots organization run by and for the trans

community, Trans Lifeline offers a crisis hotline and offers microgrants to help people who are transgender pay the legal fees to change their gender identity on documents to match their gender.

The Trevor Project
PO Box 69232
West Hollywood, CA 90069
(866) 488-7386
Website: https://www.thetrevorproject.org
Facebook: @TheTrevorProject
Twitter and Instagram: @trevorproject
YouTube: @thetrevorproject
The Trevor Projects runs a crisis and suicide prevention hotline for LGBTQ+ youth. The organization also provides a judgment-free community for LGBTQ+ youth to talk, text, and form community in their online social space.

FOR FURTHER READING

Bongiovanni, Archie, Tristan Jimerson, and Ari Yarwood. *A Quick & Easy Guide to They/Them Pronouns*. Portland, OR: Limerence Press, 2018.

Heitkamp, Kristina Lyn. *Gay-Straight Alliances: Networking with Other Teens and Allies*. New York, NY: Rosen Publishing. 2018.

Hoffman-Fox, Dara. *You and Your Gender Identity: A Guide to Discovery*. New York, NY: Skyhorse Publishing, 2017.

Huegel, Kelly. *LGBT: The Survival Guide for Lesbian, Gay, Bisexual, Transgender, and Questioning Teens*. Minneapolis, MN: Free Spirit Publishing Inc., 2018.

Light, Kate. *Gender Identity: The Search for Self*. New York, NY: Lucent Press, 2017.

Mardell, Ashley. *The ABC's of LGBT+*. Coral Gables, FL: Mango Media Inc., 2016.

McGrody, Ellen. *Coping with Gender Dysphoria*. New York, NY: The Rosen Publishing Group, Inc., 2018.

Ogden, Charlie. *Identity and Gender*. New York, NY: Crabtree Publishing Company, 2017.

Pessin-Whedbee, Brook, and Naomi Bardoff. *Who Are You? The Kid's Guide to Gender Identity*. Philadelphia, PA: Jessica Kingsley Publishers, 2017.

Petrikowski, Nicki Peter. *Gender Identity*. New York, NY: Rosen Publishing. 2014.

Testa, Rylan Jay, Deborah Coolhart, and Jayme Peta. *The Gender Quest Workbook: A Guide for Teens and Young Adults Exploring Gender Identity*. Oakland, CA: New Harbinger Publications, 2016.

Associated Press. "When 58 Gender Choices Aren't
    Enough: Facebook Launches 'Fill in the Blank' Op-
    tion for Users." *Daily Mail*, February 26, 2015. https://
    www.dailymail.co.uk/sciencetech/article-2970681
    /Facebook-adds-new-gender-option-users
    -blank.html.
Ballou, Adrian. "10 Myths About Non-Binary People It's
    Time to Unlearn." Everyday Feminism, December 6,
    2014. https://everydayfeminism.com/2014/12
    /myths-non-binary-people.
Brammer, John Paul. " Native American 'Two Spirit'
    Uses Drag to Connect to His Roots." NBC News,
    July 13, 2016. https://www.nbcnews.com/feature
    /nbc-out/native-american-two-spirit-uses-drag
    -connect-his-roots-n608591.
CBS News. "Gender-The Space Between,"
    March 29, 2017. https://www.youtube.com
    /watch?v=ZFWrzw9szt8.
Cummings, William. "When Asked Their Sex, Some Are
    Going with Option 'X'." *USA Today*, June 21, 2017.
    https://www.usatoday.com/story/news/2017/06/21
    /third-gender-option-non-binary/359260001.
Daley, Dean. "Misgendering, a Not so Silent Killer." *The
    Chronicle*, March 24, 2017. https://chronicle.durham
    -college.ca/2017/03/misgendering-not-silent-killer.
Dieker, Nicole. "How to Use Gender Neutral Pronouns"
    Lifehacker, December 19, 2017. https://lifehacker
    .com/how-to-use-gender-neutral-pronouns
    -1821239054.

Goldfarb, Anna. "Five People on Their Favorite Things About Being Nonbinary." *Vice*, June 1, 2018. https://www.vice.com/en_us/article/8xe87z/five-people-on-their-favorite-things-about-being-nonbinary.

Graves, Liz. "Rainbow Baskets Celebrate Two Spirits." *The Mount Desert Islander*, July 14, 2017. https://www.mdislander.com/living/rainbow-baskets-celebrate-two-spirits.

Greenfield, Beth. "Don't Try to Label This Actor a 'Woman' or 'Man'." Yahoo! Lifestyle, March 22, 2018. https://www.yahoo.com/lifestyle/dont-try-label-actor-woman-man-141258358.html.

Logan, Yan. "Why Being a Nonbinary Is Tough." Medium, May 25, 2017. https://medium.com/@yanlogan/why-being-a-non-binary-is-tough-7c12a7c61d03.

Lopez, German. "Gender Is Not Just Male or Female. Twelve People Across the Gender Spectrum Explain Why." Vox. Updated October 11, 2016. https://www.vox.com/identities/2016/9/28/12660752/gender-binary-spectrum-queer.

Mamone, Trav. "Yes, Non-Binary People Experience Gender Dysphoria Too." Everyday Feminism, November 12, 2017. https://everydayfeminism.com/2017/11/non-binary-gender-dysphoria-too.

Necessary, Terra. "Rebecca Sugar Opens Up About Being Non-binary." Pride, July 18, 2018. https://www.pride.com/comingout/2018/7/18/rebecca-sugar-opens-about-being-non-binary.

Papisova, Vera. "Here's What It Means When You Don't Identify as a Girl or a Boy." Teen Vogue, February 12, 2016. https://www.teenvogue.com.

Romano, Nick. "*Steven Universe* Creator Has Done More for LGBTQ Visibility Than You Might Know." *Entertainment Weekly*, August 13, 2018. https://ew.com/tv/2018/08/13/steven-universe-rebecca-sugar-lgbtq-cartoons.

Samin, Suzanne. "12 Questions About Non-Binary Gender Identity You've Been Afraid to Ask, And Real Answers." Bustle, June 10, 2015. https://www.bustle.com/articles/74316-12-questions-about-non-binary-gender-identity-youve-been-afraid-to-ask-and-real-answers

Serrao, Nivea. "*Doctor Who* Recap: 'World Enough and Time'." *Entertainment Weekly*, June 24, 2017. https://ew.com/recap/doctor-who-season-10-episode-11/2.

Tate, Allison. "Asia Kate Dillon Explains Gender-Nonbinary to Ellen." *The Advocate*, March 21, 2017. https://www.advocate.com/arts-entertainment/2017/3/21/asia-kate-dillon-explains-gender-nonbinary-ellen.

Valens, Ana. "A Guide to Understanding Cisgender Privilege." Daily Dot, March 5, 2018. https://www.dailydot.com/irl/what-is-cisgender.

ABOUT THE AUTHOR

Anita Louise McCormick is the author of many books. Her previous titles for Rosen Publishing include *Rosa Parks and the Montgomery Bus Boycott* (Spotlight on the Civil Rights Movement) and *The Native American Struggle in United States History*. McCormick identifies as a nonbinary gender-fluid trans person and is enthusiastic about working to increase public awareness and understanding of nonconforming gender identities.

PHOTO CREDITS

Cover martinedoucet/E+/Getty Images; back cover Photo by marianna armata/Moment/Getty Images; p. 5 Albert L. Ortega/Getty Images; pp. 7, 18, 28, 38 akinbostanci/E+/Getty Images; p. 8 Monkey Business Images/Shutterstock.com; p. 8 Monkey Business Images/Shutterstock.com; pp. 9, 34, 37 © AP Images; p. 12 kali9/E+/Getty Images; p. 14 Rushay Booysen/EyeEm/Getty Images; p. 15 PeopleImages/E+/Getty Images; p. 19 JGI/Jamie Grill/Getty Images; p. 21 Andrew Toth /Getty Images; p. 23 Steve Zak Photography/Getty Images; p. 26 Karl Gehring/Denver Post/Getty Images; p. 29 Elke Meitzel /Moment/Getty Images; p. 32 Julia Sanders/Shutterstock .com; p.36 Justin Sullivan/Getty Images; p. 39 James Kirkikis /Shutterstock.com; p. 42 Education & Exploration 3/Alamy Stock Photo; p. 45 Brian de Rivera Simon/Getty Images; p. 47 SolStock/E+/Getty Images; p. 50 sturti/E+/Getty Images.

Design: Michael Moy; Layout: Tahara Anderson; Editor: Jennifer Landau; Photo Researcher: Sherri Jackson